COVER PICTURE: A "palmar" of *Copernicia tectorum* in the Llanos of Calabozo, Venezuela.

The nature of VENEZUELA is simply amazing! Wherever you go, you will find lots of beautiful scenery and of course an amazing flora. The Andean mountains have a great variation of temperature and humidity. In the highest part of the Andes, the "páramos" have plants adapted to this weather. The best adaptive expression of these areas is undoubtedly the typical "frailejón" (*Espeletia*) (figures 1 and 2).

At lowest altitudes, in the Andes and other mountain ranges, the cloud forest reigns. A large number of beautiful flowering plants live in this habitat, such as the vine *Bomarea bredemeyerana* (figures 3 and 4), the exquisite *Heliconia meridensis* (figures 5 and 6), with its complex inflorescences with red bracts, yellow flowers and blue fruits, or *Govenia superba,* a terrestrial orchid (figure 7).

In a mosaic with the forest, mountain savannas have curious plants, such as *Schoenocaulon officinale* (figure 8) and *Fourcraea humboldtiana* (figure 9).

At the lowest altitudes, the Llanos are the gigantic Venezuelan savannas.

In the seasonally flooded areas of the Llanos, the "palma llanera" (*Copernicia tectorum*) forms typical landscapes (figure 10), which always influence the fantastic folk music of these great plains. The high palm *Mauritia flexuosa* forms groups in marshes called "morichales" (figure 11).

In other very sunny humid soils, the beautiful yellow flowered *Canna glauca* grows in dense groups (figure 12).

In the drier areas of the Llanos, is the presence of the "chaparro" (*Curatella americana*) (figures 13 and 14) that gives its appearance so characteristic to the landscape. Beneath the shade offered by small groups of trees grow interesting plants such as *Dorstenia brasiliensis* (figure 15).

In the humid tropical forest, or in the gallery forest of drier places, lives the glorious bulbous plant *Hymenocallis tubiflora* (figure 16).

The BASQUE COUNTRY, with its unique bronze and green mountains! (Figures 17 and 18). With a winter season that prepares an explosive flowering of many plants before the leaves have appeared in the deciduous trees (such as *Fagus sylvatica,* figures 19 and 33) and shrubs of the forests. As *Prunus avium* (figures 25 and 26) with its white virginal flowers. It is also the time when trees bearing catkins bloom, especially *Corylus avellana* (figure 22) and *Salix atrocinerea* (figures 28 and 29).

In the meadows, at the end of winter and at the beginning of spring, *Narcissus bulbocodium* blooms (figure 24).

Latter, many plants flower, such as *Cytisus scoparius* (figure 21) and *Sysimbrium austriacum* (figures 31 and 32) both with yellow flowers. The same for *Clematis vitalba* (figure 20) and *Stellaria holostea* (figure 23), with white flowers. In addition, *Chrysosplenium alternifolium*, a small green and yellow plant that forms living carpets bordering some small sunny streams (figure 30).

A frequent grass, of exquisite inflorescence, is *Agrostis capillaris* (figure 27).

On the Basque coast, the immaculate white flowers of the bulbous plant *Pancratium maritimum* (figures 34 and 35) will impress you.

VENEZUELA

Figure 1. Andean mountains. Mérida.

Figure 2. *Espeletia* in the Andean mountains.
Mérida.

Figures 3 and 4. *Bomarea bredemeyerana*. Cloud forest. Mérida.

Figure 5. *Heliconia meridensis*. Cloud forest. Lara.

Figure 6. *Heliconia meridensis*. Cloud forest. Lara.

Figure 7. *Govenia superba.* Cloud forest. Miranda.

Figure 8. *Schoenocaulon officinale*. Montane savannah. Miranda.

Figure 9. *Fourcraea humboldtiana*. Montane savannah. Miranda.

Figure 10. A "palmar" of *Copernicia tectorum*. Guárico.

Figure 11. A "morichal" of *Mauritia flexuosa*. Guárico.

Figure 12. *Canna glauca*. Guárico.

Figure 13. *Curatella americana*. Guárico.

Figure 14. *Curatella americana*. Guárico.

Figure 15. *Dorstenia brasiliensis*. Guárico.

Figure 16. *Hymenocallis tubiflora*. Miranda.

THE BASQUE COUNTRY

Figures 17 and 18. Mountains of Valcarlos.

Figure 19. A *Fagus sylvatica* forest on a limestone soil. Béhorléguy.

Figure 20. *Clematis vitalba*. Louhossoa.

Figure 21. *Cytisus scoparius*. Valcarlos.

Figure 22. *Corylus avellana.* Bayonne.

Figure 23. *Stellaria holostea*. Valcarlos.

Figure 24. *Narcissus bulbocodium*. St-Pée-sur-Nivelle.

Figure 25. *Prunus avium* blooming. St-Jean-Pied-de-Port.

Figure 26. *Prunus avium* blooming. Valcarlos.

Figure 27. The grass *Agrostis capillaris*.
Roncesvalles.

Figures 28 and 29. *Salix atrocinerea* blooming. Valcarlos.

Figure 30. *Chrysosplenium alternifolium*. Valcarlos.

Figures 31 and 32. *Sysimbrium austriacum*. Valcarlos.

Figure 33: A *Fagus sylvatica* forest. Valcarlos.

Figures 34 and 35. *Pancratium maritimum*. Anglet.